11/14

Paper it!

50 home decor and gift ideas using scrapbook papers

Martingale®
& COMPANY

Paper It! 50 Home Decor and Gift Ideas
Using Scrapbook Papers
© 2008 by Martingale & Company®

Martingale & Company
20205 144th Ave. NE
Woodinville, WA 98072-8478 USA
www.martingale-pub.com

Printed in China
13 12 11 10 09 08   8 7 6 5 4 3 2 1

Library of Congress Cataloging-in-Publication Data
Library of Congress Control Number: 2008031696

ISBN: 978-1-56477-888-8

CREDITS

President & CEO • Tom Wierzbicki
Publisher • Jane Hamada
Editorial Director • Mary V. Green
Managing Editor • Tina Cook
Technical Editor • Dawn Anderson
Copy Editor • Marcy Heffernan
Design Director • Stan Green
Production Manager • Regina Girard
Illustrator • Laurel Strand
Cover & Text Designer • Shelly Garrison
Photographer • Brent Kane

MISSION STATEMENT

Dedicated to providing quality products
and service to inspire creativity.

SCRAPBOOK PAPERS USED IN BOOK DESIGN

- Autumn Leaves, a Division of Creativity Inc.: C'est Pink #7001 by Rhonna Farrer

- Basic Grey: Blush, BLU 654 Charmed; Pattern Paper, Two Scoops/Ice Cream Parlor/TSC 1058; Periphery, Merlot PIP 912; Pheobe, Sausalito PHE 763; Scarlet's Letter; Rapture SCR 806; Stella Ruby, London Sunset STE 728

- Fancy Pants Designs, Inc.: Appealing 863 by Michelle Coleman; Bluebell 837 by Nancie Rowe-Janitz

- K & Company: Rhapsody Garden, Collage, Thermo Glitter 643077 655508.

- Memory Box, Inc.: Homespun Collection, Slipcover

- My Mind's Eye: Bohemia Bliss Love of My Life #BH2050; Bohemia Bluebird Birthday; Bohemia Bungalow Our Family Medallion/Light Orange #BH2158; Kaleidoscope Birthday Boy Dots/Mint Paper #KS3032; Kaleidoscope On the Shore Dots/Mint Paper # KS3071

Contents

Introduction

Whether you want to give a unique gift, help kids store their stuff, accessorize your home, or pamper yourself, just *Paper It!* Now you can use your scrapbooking papers and embellishments in exciting new ways that range from practical to whimsical, with ideas for young and old.

Going to a bridal shower? Bring the bride a retro-inspired recipe binder—and slip in your favorite recipe! Hosting a baby shower? Thrill the new mom with an embellished nursery tote or grapevine wreath for Baby's room.

Have a child in your life? Kids just want to have fun, so we've included ideas to make work fun! Create the "to do" board on page 39, put tasks on movable disks, and let little ones enjoy "doing their disks." With the bright school-supply box on page 5, you'll encourage youngsters to stay organized and stash away their school tools.

Eager to spruce up the house? The cherry-themed accessories on page 15 will quickly cheer up the kitchen. Then you can create the spice bottle storage unit on page 40 to add extra zest. And that's just the beginning—in this book you'll find easy-to-make projects to organize and appoint any room.

Want to make a little something just for you? You'll love personalizing your work space with colorful desk and supply organizers. And just picture yourself reaching for your favorite publications in the stylish magazine holder on page 36. Spend a creative day, and at day's end you can spend pleasant moments placing your beads and bangles—or gems and jewels—in the jewelry box on page 12.

We've provided loads of inspiring photos. So you might want to start with the beribboned journal on page 12 to record your schemes, dreams, and ideas—including ideas for even more ways to *Paper It!*

Child's School-Supply Box

Create a custom-crafted child's school-supply box for pencils, crayons, markers, glue, scissors or other school supplies. This box is sure to brighten any child's day.

By Gina Hamann

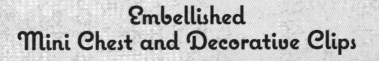

Embellished
Mini Chest and Decorative Clips

Stash everyday items in a set of stylish wooden drawers covered with eye-catching patterned papers. List the contents of each drawer with a fancy stamped label embellished with gemstones. Use the clothespins, turned into cute clips, to organize stacks of notes, to do lists, bills, and coupons. Embellished with a stamped tag, fabric-covered brads, or a row of gemstones, these clips are a far cry from their humble roots.

By Saralyn Ewald

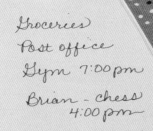

Groceries
Post office
Gym 7:00 pm

Brian - chess
4:00 pm

Decorative Tray

Make this decorative patchwork tray to use as a fun conversation piece! Display it on a cocktail table or in the kitchen for a creative touch.

By Nicole Johnson

Embellished Mailbox

Store all your postage needs in this handy mailbox! Decorate it to match your decor and display it where you do all of your correspondence. Create custom file folders to coordinate.

By Nicole Johnson

Wreath for Baby's Room

Decorate baby's nursery with a grapevine wreath dressed in painted chipboard flowers, embossed metal frames, and tags tied with ribbon. Buttons, covered in a coat of glitter, add eye-catching sparkle in the centers of the chipboard flowers.

By Saralyn Ewald

Nursery Tote

Keep baby's items contained in a wooden flatware caddy turned nursery tote! Sweetly patterned papers, playful ribbon, and a die-cut label embellished with pink glitter lend oh-so-cute charm. Fill this tote with necessities for the mom-to-be, and present it as the ultimate baby shower gift!

By Saralyn Ewald

Composition Book Journal

Create the perfect place to record thoughts, ideas, notes, and memories! This journal features a ribbon tie created by tucking ribbon under the decorative papers that adorn the cover.

By Saralyn Ewald

Jewelry Box

Drawers covered with patterned paper and knobs adorned with fabric-covered brads turn a plain jewelry box into a one-of-a-kind gem. A few delicate branches and a sweet little bird, all cut from decorative papers, add the finishing touch.

By Saralyn Ewald

12

Cowboy Clock and Photo Frame

These room accessories are the perfect addition to any little cowboy's room. Denim- and bandana-patterned paper and a vintage cowboy image give the clock a Western feel. Western-themed patterned papers and painted chipboard letters give a plain photo frame a custom-crafted finish.

By Jennifer Ulrick

13

Spiral-Bound Diary

Record secrets, dreams, wishes, and hopes in a spiral-bound scrapbook turned diary. The ribbon tie guards the diary's contents while adding a feminine touch. Layers of patterned papers and dimensional embellishments add color and interest to what once was a plain black cover.

By Saralyn Ewald

Decorative Storage Boxes and Note Holder

Tuck barrettes, jewelry, trinkets, and treasures inside these one-of-a-kind decorative boxes. Colorful patterned papers and sparkling accents transform simple papier-mâché boxes into a cute storage solution. Transform an oversized wooden clothespin into a coordinating note holder or photo clip.

By Saralyn Ewald

Birthdays
• Feb. 23 - Kayla
• March 4 - Becca
• March 13 - Josh
• June 2 - Megan
• July 15 - Kaitlyn
• Sept. 21 - Lily
• Nov. 6 - Alyssa
• Dec. 8 - Jessie

friends

Cherry Kitchen Accessories

Create retro-inspired kitchen accessories with vintage-style papers and cherry motifs that you'll be proud to keep on your kitchen counter. The utensil and napkin holders are accented with cherry tags and red gingham ribbons. A red metal nameplate and more cherries finish the recipe box.

By Saralyn Ewald

Girl's Jewelry Box

Make a decorative place for jewelry and other small keepsakes by embellishing a plain jewelry box with paint and patterned paper. Coordinating ribbon, a painted chipboard frame, flowers, and lots of sparkly gems make it perfect for any girl's special treasures.

By Jennifer Ulrick

Flower Mobile

Create a unique piece of decor to add a bit of whimsy to a girl's bedroom. Simply decorate unfinished wooden shapes with paint, patterned paper, and sparkly embellishments, and clip them onto the wire mobile. Use alternate shapes and colors to accent any room in your home.

By Jennifer Ulrick

The beautiful calendar pages and attractive tabs make the interior of this planner almost as stunning as the exterior. This project makes a wonderful gift!

Planner, Coupon, and Address Books

Keep track of everything with this beautiful set of organizational books! The planner has pockets for every month containing tags for to do lists and envelopes for receipts. Store your coupons in style in a converted photo album complete with decorative tabs, and keep addresses handy in a one-of-kind address book made to match.

By Nicole Johnson

19

Seaside Frames

Display your favorite seaside memories in a trio of embellished frames. Create a mosaic "Ocean" frame—no grout required! This mosaic uses pieces of patterned paper, paint, and chipboard letters to create a design that captures a laid-back beach feel. Buttons, reminiscent of sea glass, cover a second frame, while layered patterned papers, including a strip cut in a wave shape, decorate the third frame.

By Saralyn Ewald

Pink Organizers

Organize your paid bills, receipts, take-home menus, and other household items in the cleverly decorated file box at right. Coordinate it with the bill file and everything binder to create a total home-organization system. These are so pretty, you won't mind them sitting out on display!

By Nicole Johnson

Since this box came with a lip to accommodate hanging folders, a paper-covered chipboard strip, cut slightly wider than the folders, was secured to the front and back of each. The ends of the chipboard strips rest on the lip of the box, allowing the folders to hang.

Three-Ring Recipe Binder

Organize your favorite recipes (or take-out menus!) in this retro-inspired three-ring binder. The plain chipboard cover becomes a blast from the past with gingham-patterned paper, vintage-inspired labels, and cheerful oversized rickrack trim.

By Saralyn Ewald

Coffee Clock

Get your coffee fix around the clock! The face of this wooden clock is covered with layered patterned-paper circles, and the hours are marked with a mix of chipboard numbers and coffee-themed tags.

By Saralyn Ewald

Desk and Supply Organizers

These colorful items will keep your desk organized yet stylish. The desk organizer is accented with family photos for a personal touch.

By Christine Falk

Key Hook and Photo Display

Decorate a plain white piece of wall decor to create a one-of-a-kind piece of art for your home; simply add some patterned paper, paper-covered chipboard shapes, and metal accents. Personalize your wall art by adding your favorite photo!

By Jennifer Ulrick

Welcome Photo Tray

Why should a tray only be used to carry objects?
Select a favorite photo; then decorate an unfinished
tray to create a welcoming piece of wall art for your
home. The patterned paper gives the background a
tiled mosaic feel, while buttons, chipboard shapes,
and a silk flower give the surface dimension.

By Jennifer Ulrick

Embellished Bulletin Board
with Coordinating Tacks

Display favorite photos, important notes, and to do lists on
a bulletin board that's been framed with playful patterned
papers and stamped with inspiring words. This project is
perfect for a child's room, or you can select paper and
embellishments to match any room of the house. Don't
forget the coordinating tacks!

By Saralyn Ewald

Decorated Papier-Mâché Letter "E"

Customize a papier-mâché letter to match the personality (or bedroom decor) of a special child in your life—or use multiple decorated letters to create a word to hang on the wall. Patterned papers, cut into strips and adhered to the letter's surface, quickly transform the letter from plain to playful.

By Saralyn Ewald

Turned Table Leg Photo Display

Turn a found object into a creative display for photos and other ephemera. Add dimensional flowers and ribbons with clips, and this piece is sure to turn heads!

By Nicole Johnson

Magnet Board

Display important notes and photos attractively on this creative magnet board made with a cabinet door and galvanized flashing hidden behind patterned paper.

By Nicole Johnson

Stylish Organizers and Checkbook Cover

Keep all of your important dates stored in one place! This easy-to-use file houses one tabbed card for each month with space to record special anniversaries or birthdays. Since it is a perpetual calendar, you can use it year after year. Craft a complementary book for notes and a decorative checkbook cover to complete a coordinated set.

By Nicole Johnson

Scraplight

Shed some light on your favorite memories! Position a scrapbook page featuring small versions of your favorite photos, a patterned paper heart, and coordinating letters between the two layers of this light, and your memories are ready for illumination.

By Saralyn Ewald

Embellished Lampshade

Use your favorite paper-crafting supplies and techniques to add a personal touch to your home decor. The shade is personalized with an over-sized rub-on initial and trimmed with ribbon and chipboard flowers.

By Saralyn Ewald

35

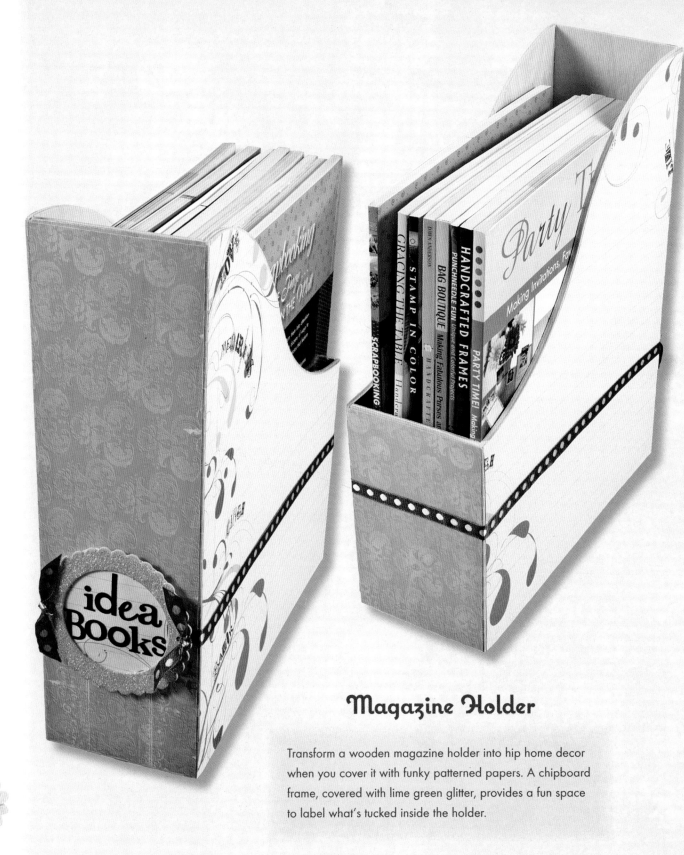

idea
Books

STAMP IN COLOR

GRACING THE TABLE

SCRAPBOOKING

HANDCRAFTED FRAMES
PUNCHNEEDLE FUN Unique and Colorful Projects

BAG BOUTIQUE Making Fabulous Purses an

PARTY TIME! Making

Party Ti
Making Invitations, Fav

Magazine Holder

Transform a wooden magazine holder into hip home decor when you cover it with funky patterned papers. A chipboard frame, covered with lime green glitter, provides a fun space to label what's tucked inside the holder.

By Saralyn Ewald

Keepsake Box

Trimmed with a border of buttons and eye-catching gemstones, this little keepsake box is a great place to store trinkets and treasures. Make this box your own when you personalize it with a glitter-covered chipboard initial.

By Saralyn Ewald

"Family" Word Display

Your word display can be used as the focal point on a fireplace mantel or shelf, or it can be hung on a wall to accessorize a room. Use the letters of a child's name to decorate a bedroom or create a seasonal message for a holiday.

By Gina Hamann

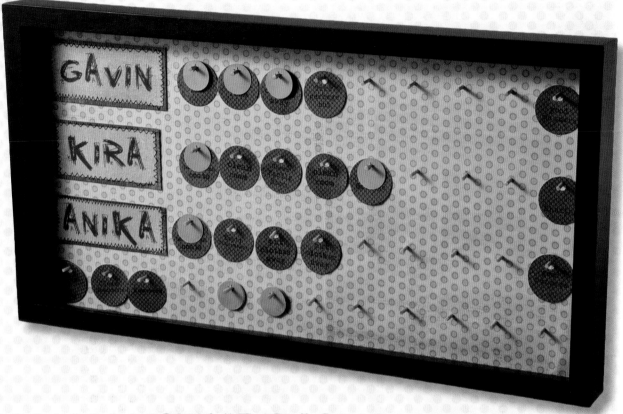

Kids' "To Do" Board

The kids' to do board is a way to keep track of daily responsibilities. Each day choose the tasks to be completed and hang the task disks next to each child's name. When the task is complete, hang a completion disk over the task. Reward accomplishments with reward disks using the extra pegs at the end of each row.

By Gina Hamann

The jars are labeled:

shaped brads · conchos · hinges · ribbon charms · metallic brads

colored brads · decorative brads · paper clips · metallic eyelets · rhinestone brads

Spice Bottle Storage Unit

Cleverly covered with paper and labeled, these jars
are the perfect accessory to store and display your
small embellishments!

By Nicole Johnson

Lazy Susan Craft-Supply Center

Functional and decorative, this lazy Susan uses labeled metal buckets as crafting supply bins. A turned spindle in the center adds a bit of height as well as charm.

By Nicole Johnson

Countdown to Christmas

Create a family tradition of counting down and displaying the days until Christmas with this framed piece. The chip-board numbers are stored in an attractive coordinating tin.

By Nicole Johnson

"Joy" Framed

Spread some holiday cheer with this elegant framed art piece hanging from a beautiful ribbon.

By Nicole Johnson

Craft-Supply Box and Paintbrush Holder

Craft-supply boxes keep small amounts of supplies organized. By using the same-sized box for each category of supplies, you can keep your storage area neat and attractive. A paintbrush holder is one more way to stay organized. This container also works well for holding pencils, markers, scissors, and other similar tools.

By Gina Hamann

Materials and Instructions

Page 5
CHILD'S SCHOOL-SUPPLY BOX

Materials

8¼" x 6¼" x 2" printed box with magnetic closure, corners – Daisy D's

Patterned paper: K & Company – Amy Butler; Cosmo Cricket

Brads: Making Memories

Flowers: Prima Marketing

Label holder

Decorative chipboard letters – Pressed Petals; K & Company

Ribbon and rickrack trim

Self-adhesive gemstones

Metal photo corners

Personal photo

White craft glue

How to:

Cut patterned paper to fit on the front of the box and adhere in place. Cut ⅝" strips of patterned paper and adhere to the sides of the box to create a border at one edge. Adhere gemstones to the centers of the flowers on the patterned paper and every ½" around the side border. Embellish the letters with gemstones and an assortment of ribbons and rickrack, either glued onto or tied around the letters. Adhere the letters to the box. Adhere a photo to the label holder and install brads in the holes. Adhere the label holder and metal corners to the box. Install brads in the layered flower centers and adhere to the box. Insert a ribbon through the pre-installed grommets on one side of the box and knot the ends of the ribbon on the inside to create a handle.

Page 7
EMBELLISHED MINI CHEST
AND DECORATIVE CLIPS

Materials
(for one chest and multiple clips)

14" x 10¼" mini chest with five drawers: IKEA – Fira

Wooden flat-sided clothespins

Patterned paper and fabric-covered brads: K & Company – Amy Butler Belle Collection

White cardstock

Lime grosgrain ribbon

Self-adhesive gemstones

Label stamps: Paper Salon – Monogram Builder

Clear acrylic stamp block

Alphabet stamps: Stampendous – Small Typewriter Alphabet

Brown and magenta inkpads

Decoupage medium: Plaid – Matte Mod Podge

Superglue – Future Glue Gel

Other: ⅛" hole punch, foam brush, and wire snips

How to:

Embellished Mini Chest. To cover the drawer fronts, cut patterned papers to size, joining the papers for the larger drawers as necessary. Apply Mod Podge to the drawer fronts and adhere the papers. Cover the outside of the chest with paper, securing it with Mod Podge. Stamp five magenta labels onto white cardstock, and then stamp the contents of each drawer inside the labels with brown ink. Let dry, and then cut out the labels, cutting off the left side of each image. Adhere the labels to the drawer fronts. Apply two gemstones along the right side of each label. If desired, cover the drawer fronts with one or more coats of Mod Podge to protect the chest from the wear of daily use.

Decorative Clips. Cut ⅜"-wide strips from the patterned papers and trim the strips to the necessary lengths. Adhere the strips to the front of the clothespins using Mod Podge. Adhere three gemstones to one of the clothespins. Use wire snips to remove the prongs from two brads, taking care to secure the prongs to prevent injury from them flying about. Using superglue, adhere the brads to a second clothespin. Stamp a magenta label onto white cardstock, and then stamp "to do" with brown ink at the center of the label. Let dry, and then cut out the label and punch a ⅛" hole on the side. Wrap ribbon around the front of a third clothespin, thread the label onto the ribbon, and secure with a knot.

Page 8
DECORATIVE TRAY

Materials

13" x 19" wood tray: Winsome

Patterned paper: Chatterbox – Sky Floral Quilt, Sky Bias Plaid, Vase Bouquet, Burgundy Flowers; Making Memories – Ava Loopy Stripe (reverse side)

Scalloped paper circle: Bazzill Basics – Medium Scallop Circle Brown

Scalloped note card: Archiver's

Decorative cards: My Mind's Eye – Tres Jolie Friends and Cousins

Rub-ons: Fiskars – Heidi Grace Designs Harvest Row

Inkpad: Clearsnap – Colorbox Fluid Chalk Chestnut Roan

Templates: small flower, medium flower, leaf, and scroll (pages 61 and 62)

Decoupage medium: Plaid – Matte Mod Podge

¾" diameter circle punch: EK Success

How to:

Cut a 10⅛" x 12" rectangle of Sky Floral Quilt paper; distress the edges by rubbing them with the inkpad, and then apply the corner image and circle flower image rub-ons to the top left corner. Use Mod Podge to adhere the paper to the left side of the tray. Cut one 1½" x 8" strip and one ¾" x 12" strip from the Burgundy Flowers paper. Cut a 1⅞" x 7½" strip from the reverse side of the Ava Loopy Stripe. Cut a ⅞" x 9" strip from the Sky Bias Plaid paper. Cut a 1⅞" x 11¾" strip from Vase Bouquet paper. Rub the edges of all the cut papers and the edges of the scalloped note card with the inkpad. Add the scroll rub-on to the scalloped note card. Trim the brown scalloped circle cardstock to 5¾" wide at the center and 10⅛" long. Arrange the cut paper pieces and decorative cards as shown and adhere with Mod Podge.

Using the templates on pages 61 and 62, trace one medium flower, one small flower, one leaf, and one scroll onto patterned papers and cut out. Punch a ¾" circle from

45

paper. Rub the edges of the flower pieces with the inkpad. Fold the leaf in half and rub the fold with the inkpad. Layer the flower pieces as shown and adhere with Mod Podge to the brown scalloped paper. Coat the inside bottom of the tray with Mod Podge to protect the paper.

Page 9
EMBELLISHED MAILBOX
Materials

14" wide x 9" high x 5" deep mailbox: Steel City Corp–Coventry

Spray paint: Rust-Oleum–Painter's Touch Espresso Satin

Patterned paper: Chatterbox–Sky Floral Quilt, Sky Bias Plaid, Vase Bouquet

Chipboard letters (m, a, i, and l): BasicGrey–Undressed Chipboard Monograms

Decorative card: My Mind's Eye–Tres Jolie Smile

Inkpad: Clearsnap–Colorbox Fluid Chalk Chestnut Roan

Buttons

Ribbon: American Crafts

Tag: Office Max

Manila file folders, letter size: Office Max

Marker: EK Success– Zig Millennium (.01 mm tip) Black

Templates: large flower, medium flower, and small flower (page 61)

Double-sided adhesive tape: 3M–Scotch ATG 714 adhesive and dispenser

Mini double-sided adhesive glue dots: Glue Dots International

Liquid glue: US ArtQuest–Perfect Paper Adhesive

Tab die and die-cutting tool: QuicKutz–Tabs and Squeeze Die-Cutting hand tool

Other: Sandpaper

How to:

Paint the mailbox following the manufacturer's directions and set aside to dry. Using double-sided tape, adhere a 4¾" border of Vase Bouquet paper to the lower portion of the mailbox, piecing as necessary. (Place the front seam where it will be concealed by the letter "l.") Trim the Sky Bias Plaid into ¼" strips. Adhere the strips (Sky Bias Plaid side down) to the mailbox along the top and bottom edges of the Vase Bouquet paper. Trace the chipboard letters in reverse onto the back of the Sky Floral Quilt paper, cut out, and adhere the

paper letters to the chipboard with Perfect Paper Adhesive. Sand and then rub the edges of the letters with the inkpad for a distressed finish.

Write the word "Supplies" on the tag and rub the edges with the inkpad. Tie a piece of ribbon around the "l," securing the tag to the letter. Adhere the chipboard letters to the front of the mailbox. Trace one large, two medium, and one small flower onto patterned papers using the templates on page 61. Cut the flowers out, and rub the edges with the inkpad. Layer the flower pieces as desired and secure with mini glue dots. Roll the petals around a pencil to create dimension. Adhere buttons to the centers of the flowers. Write the words "stamps," "envelopes," and "labels" onto the lined Smile card. Attach the flowers and the card to the lid with glue dots.

To make the file folders, trim the file folders down to 7" and add a 1" strip of patterned paper to the top edge of each file. Punch three tabs using the tab punch. Write "stamps," "labels," and "envelopes" on the tabs. Adhere the labels to the files.

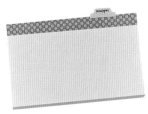

Page 10
WREATH FOR BABY'S ROOM
Materials

18" grapevine wreath

Patterned paper and decorative paper tags: K & Company–Marcella

Patterned paper: Daisy D's–Classic Baby Plaid

Chipboard tags, glitter alphabet stickers and Vintage Hip Metal Frames: Making Memories

Chipboard flowers: Maya Road

Chipboard letters (b, a, b, and y): BasicGrey

Assorted pink, yellow, and green ribbons

Light green and pink acrylic paint

White and pink glitter

Assorted buttons

Hot glue gun and glue sticks

White craft glue: Aleene's Quick Dry Tacky Glue

Crop-A-Dile Eyelet and Snap Punch: We R Memory Makers

How to:

Paint the chipboard tags green and let dry. Spell out words on each tag with glitter alphabet stickers. Cover a few chipboard flowers with patterned paper and a few with pink paint. Coat the pink and white buttons with craft glue, sprinkle glitter on top, tap off the excess, and let dry. Adhere the buttons to the centers of the flowers. Paint the chipboard letters, let dry, and then adhere in the lower-left corner of one of the metal frames. Adhere an image, cut from patterned paper, in the window of each frame. Punch a hole at the top of each frame and each chipboard flower with the Crop-A-Dile tool. Arrange all of the decorative pieces, including the coordinating paper tags, on the wreath. Thread and knot ribbon through the holes in each piece. Adhere the decorative pieces to the grapevine wreath with hot glue.

Page 11
NURSERY TOTE

Materials

9" wide x 6" deep x 12" high wooden flatware caddy

Patterned papers, flower tag, and frame: K & Company–Marcella

"BABY" printed die cut: My Mind's Eye–Tres Jolie

Chipboard flower: Maya Road

Chipboard scraps

Green polka-dot ribbon

White narrow rickrack

Pink glitter: Doodlebug Design

Decoupage medium: Plaid–Matte Mod Podge

Double-sided tape: Suze Weinberg's Wonder Tape

Fine-tip glue pen

Crop-A-Dile Eyelet and Snap Punch: We R Memory Makers

Other: foam brush

How to:

Cut patterned papers to size to line the inside of the tote. Adhere the papers to the inside of the tote using an even coat of Mod Podge. Cut patterned papers to size for the front and back of the tote and adhere in place. Cut ¾" strips of patterned paper and adhere along the upper edge of the tote front to create a border. Cut a piece of paper to wrap around the handle of the tote and secure it to the handle using a long strip of double-sided tape. Paper with a decorative border was positioned with the decorative end of the paper at one end of the handle. Then another border strip was adhered to the other end of the handle. Wrap ribbon horizontally around the center of the tote and secure it in the front with double-sided tape. Adhere a paper frame to the center front, on top of the ribbon. Use a glue pen to trace over the letters of the printed die cut, sprinkle glitter over the glue, and then tap off the excess. Let dry. Cut and adhere scraps of chipboard to cover the back of the die cut; adhere to the center of the paper frame using double-sided tape. Apply glitter to the petals of a flower tag in the same manner as for the letters; adhere the tag to the center of a chipboard flower that's been covered with patterned paper. Punch a hole through the chipboard flower using a Crop-A-Dile tool, and then tie it to the handle of the tote with a piece of ribbon and a piece of rickrack.

Page 12
COMPOSITION BOOK JOURNAL

Materials

7½" x 9¾" composition notebook

Patterned paper: My Mind's Eye–Bohemia, Bliss, Love of My Life; K & Company–Hannah Blue and Ivory; SEI–Granny's Kitchen

Glitter letter stickers: Making Memories–Shimmer Alpha Stickers

Jumbo pewter bookplate with brads: BasicGrey

Ivory acrylic paint

Blue ribbon

Decoupage medium: Plaid–Matte Mod Podge

Double-sided tape: Suze Weinberg's Wonder Tape

Hole punch: Making Memories

Other: sandpaper

How to:

Cut a 32" length of ribbon, wrap it around the outside of the book, and secure it to the cover with double-sided tape. Using Mod Podge, adhere a 6⅝" x 9¹¹⁄₁₆" piece of blue paper to the back of the book, aligning it with the open edge of the book. Trim the corners of the paper to match the book. Adhere a 7⅛" x 9¹¹⁄₁₆" piece of blue flower paper to the inside cover of the book, aligning it with the open edge of the book. Let dry, and then trim the corners. Adhere a 6⅝" x 9¹¹⁄₁₆" piece of pink paper to the front cover of the book, aligning it with the open edge of the book. Let dry, and then trim the corners. Adhere a 1" x 9¹¹⁄₁₆" strip of blue paper along the left edge of the pink paper on the journal front. Lightly sand the bookplate, paint it, and let dry. Adhere the flower-patterned paper, cut to size, behind the bookplate, and adhere letter stickers to spell "Journal" in the window. Determine the placement of the bookplate and mark the hole placement on the journal cover. Attach the bookplate by punching two holes through the cover at the marked points and installing brads through the holes.

Page 12
JEWELRY BOX
Materials

11" long x 7½" wide x 9¾" high five-drawer jewelry box: Storables

Patterned paper: K & Company–pink patterned paper, Addison Blue Gingham, and Hannah Blue and Ivory; SEI–Granny's Kitchen; Daisy D's—Red Polka-Dot

Fabric-covered brads: K & Company–Amy Butler

Templates: bird and branch (page 61)

Quick-dry tacky glue: Aleene's Quick Dry Tacky Glue

Superglue–Future Glue Gel

Other: ⅛" hole punch, paintbrush, sandpaper, wire snips

How to:

Remove the knobs from the drawers and lightly sand the drawer fronts. Use wire snips to remove the prongs from the brads. Adhere the brads to the front of the drawer knobs using superglue; set them aside to dry. Cut the papers to size to cover the drawer fronts. Determine where the screws for each drawer knob will go through the papers and punch a ⅛" hole in the papers to accommodate the screws. Working with one piece of paper at a time, brush an even coat of tacky glue on the back of the

paper and adhere to the corresponding drawer front. Cut a branch and a portion of a branch from pink paper and a bird from red paper using the templates on page 61. Adhere the cut pieces to the drawer fronts, carefully cutting and spreading the pieces apart where they overlap onto a second drawer. Cut another branch portion from blue floral paper and adhere to the top of the box. Reattach the knobs.

Page 13
COWBOY CLOCK AND PHOTO FRAME: CLOCK

Materials

14"-diameter clock

Patterned paper: Anna Griffin–Denim; Leisure Arts–Red Bandana

Cowboy Racing image: The Vintage Workshop (see "Resources" on page 63)

Foam number stamps: Making Memories

Acrylic paint: Making Memories–Shopping bag

Decoupage medium: Plaid–Matte Mod Podge

Other: foam brush, self-healing cutting mat, X-Acto knife

How to:

Carefully remove the clock hands and set aside. Cut the Denim paper into strips 3" wide. Using the foam brush, apply an even coat of Mod Podge to the front surface of the clock. Working quickly before it dries, cover the entire front surface with the Denim strips. Some of the paper will extend from the edges. Let the Mod Podge dry completely. Flip the clock paper side down onto a self-healing cutting mat. Use an X-Acto knife to trim the excess paper. Trim the Red Bandana paper to 7½" x 8½". Apply Mod Podge to the back and adhere it to the center of the clock front. As you adhere the paper in place, gently let the center clock hardware pierce through the paper. Print out the cowboy image from The Vintage Workshop following the manufacturer's instructions. Trim the printed image to 6" x 7". Center and adhere the image to the clock front, letting the center clock hardware pierce through the image. Stamp the numbers on the clock with paint. It is helpful to make a small pencil mark where each number should go before you begin. Apply a thin layer of Mod Podge to the entire front surface of the clock and let dry. Reattach the clock hands.

Page 13
COWBOY CLOCK AND PHOTO FRAME: FRAME
Materials

12" x 12" ready-to-make photo frame

Patterned paper: Creative Imaginations–Blue Bandana, Red Bandana; Imaginisce–Out on a Whim; Carolee's Creations–Howdy Words

Self-adhesive chipboard letters (c, o, w, b, o, and y): BasicGrey–Undressed Chipboard Mini Monos

Clear stamps: Fontwerks–Seeing Stars by Tia Bennett

Inkpads: Tsukineko–Brilliance Coffee Bean; Colorbox–Fluid Chalk Chestnut Roan

Decorative brads, fabric tag: Making Memories

Acrylic paint: Making Memories–Shopping Bag

Acrylic block (at least 3" x 3")

Double-sided adhesive tape: 3M–Scotch ATG 714 adhesive and dispenser

Mini double-sided adhesive glue dots: Glue Dots International

5" x 5" personal photo

Other: foam brush, wire snips

How to:

Using the foam brush, apply paint to the entire front surface of the photo frame and the chipboard letters. Set aside to dry. Rub the edges of the frame and the edges of the letters with the Chestnut Roan inkpad for a distressed look. Using the Coffee Bean inkpad and Seeing Stars stamps, randomly stamp star images to the entire front surface of the frame. Cut the blue paper to 3" x 12". Tear along one 12" side to produce a 2½" x 12" strip. Cut the Out on a Whim paper to 4" x 12". Tear along one 12" side to produce a 3½" x 12" strip. Adhere both strips to the lower portion of the frame with double-sided adhesive tape, blue strip on top. Cut a 3" square of red paper, and then cut the square once diagonally to make two triangles. Adhere a triangle to each upper corner of the frame. Cut the Howdy patterned paper to 2" x 6" and adhere to the frame. Use the wire snips to cut the prongs off of three brads, taking

care to secure the prongs to prevent injury from them flying about. Adhere the brads along the upper-right corner of the frame using glue dots. Pierce a brad through the top of the fabric tag and open the brad on the back side. Adhere the tag to the lower-left corner of the frame. Peel the backing from the self adhesive chipboard letters and adhere along the lower portion of the frame. Insert a 5" x 5" photo in the frame opening.

Page 14
SPIRAL-BOUND DIARY

Materials

9¼" x 10" spiral-bound scrapbook: Canson

Patterned papers, chipboard flower buttons, and chipboard alphabet: K & Company–Margo

Ribbons (fuchsia satin and lime polka-dot)

White craft glue: Aleene's Original Tacky Glue

Double-sided tape: Suze Weinberg's Wonder Tape

Other: paintbrush

How to:

Cut patterned papers to fit on the front and back covers, creating a contrasting border for the top front cover. Adhere a 24" piece of ribbon across the center back cover with tape. Glue patterned paper over the ribbon. Repeat on the front cover. Cut a 3½" paper square; cut it once diagonally. Adhere one half to the bottom right corner of the cover; the remaining half won't be used for this project. Cut out three flowers from floral patterned paper and adhere them along the edge of the corner paper with tape. Glue dimensional chipboard buttons in the lower-right corner. Spell out "DIARY" with chipboard letters and adhere to the cover with glue. Tie a few pieces of ribbon to the spiral binding.

Page 14
DECORATIVE STORAGE BOXES AND NOTE HOLDER

**Materials
(for two boxes and one note holder)**

2 papier-mâché boxes (one 2½" high x 4¾" wide and one 3" high x 6" wide)

1⅜" x 4⅜" x 1" clothespin: Creative Imaginations–Bare Elements Oversized Wood Clothespin

Patterned papers, chipboard buttons, and chipboard butterfly sticker: K & Company–Margo

Gemstones: Darice–Crystals

White cardstock

Alphabet stamps: Stampendous–Small Typewriter Alphabet

Inkpad: Tsukineko–VersaColor Opera Pink

Rub-on white swirl: Making Memories

Crystal knob: 7 Gypsies

Mini double-sided adhesive glue dots: Glue Dots International

White craft glue: Aleene's Original Tacky Glue

Hole punch: Making Memories

Other: circle cutter, hole punch, paintbrush

How to:

Decorative Storage Boxes. Cut patterned papers to fit on all exposed surfaces of the boxes and adhere with glue. Adhere gemstones about 1" apart to the side of the larger lid using glue dots. Working from the underside of the small lid, punch a hole through the center using the hole punch. Remove the gemstone from the center of the chipboard flower button. Adhere the button to the center of a 2" circle cut from patterned paper. Punch a hole through the center of the button and paper, and then adhere them to the center of the small lid, making sure the punched holes align. Secure the glass knob through the punched holes on the lid.

Note Holder. Cut and adhere patterned paper to the front and back surfaces of the clothespin. Apply a rub-on swirl about 1" from the top of the clip. Stamp "friends" on white cardstock and let dry. Cut the stamped letters apart and adhere them along the edge of the front of the clip. Position a chipboard butterfly sticker at the top of the swirl.

Page 15
CHERRY KITCHEN ACCESSORIES

Materials
(for one utensil holder, one napkin holder, and one recipe box)

Metal utensil holder

Metal napkin holder: OXO – Napkin Pinch

Metal recipe box

Patterned papers and border stickers: My Minds Eye – Tres Jolie

White and brown cardstock

Red acrylic paint

Red gingham ribbon

Red buttons

Red metal nameplate

Alphabet stamps: Stampendous – Small Typewriter Alphabet

Red inkpad

Metal brads

Decoupage medium: Plaid – Matte Mod Podge

Double-sided adhesive foam dots: Plaid – All Night Media Pop Dots

Double-sided tape: Suze Weinberg's Wonder Tape

Liquid glue: Tombow – Mono Metal

Crop-A-Dile Eyelet and Snap Punch: We R Memory Makers

Other: ¼" hole punch, corner rounder punch tool, and foam brush

How to:

Cherry Utensil Holder. Cut red paper to fit around the utensil holder, piecing as necessary. Apply strips of Wonder Tape to the back of each piece of paper, around the edges. Starting with the larger piece, cover the remaining paper area with an even coat of Mono Metal liquid glue, and then wrap the paper around the utensil holder. Repeat with any remaining pieces of patterned paper to cover the holder. Using Mod Podge, adhere a 1½"-wide strip of yellow paper over the red paper

to create a stripe. Piece the yellow stripe as necessary to create a continuous stripe. Cover the adhered paper with one or more coats of Mod Podge to protect it from the wear of daily use. Cut a 3⅛" circle from patterned paper and a 2⅞" circle from white cardstock. Paint the edge of the white circle with red paint and adhere at the center of the patterned circle. Adhere two buttons, two cherry stems cut from brown cardstock, and a leaf cut from green paper to the white circle. Punch a ¼" hole at the top of the circle. Wrap red gingham ribbon around the holder, over the yellow stripe. Thread the tag onto the ribbon; secure with a knot. Position a couple of foam dots behind the tag to hold it in place.

Cherry Napkin Holder. Cut two 5½" x 6⅛" pieces of patterned paper to cover the front and back of the napkin holder. Apply strips of tape to the back of the paper, around the edges. Working with one piece at a time, cover the remaining paper area with an even coat of Mono Metal liquid glue, and then apply the paper to one side of the napkin holder. Repeat with the second piece of patterned paper, covering the second side of the holder. Cover both sides with one or more coats of Mod Podge to protect them from the wear of daily use. Cut a tag from patterned paper and a 2" circle from white cardstock. Paint the edge of the white circle with red paint and adhere to the tag overlapping the edge of the tag on one side. Trim the excess even with the edge of the tag. Adhere two buttons, two cherry stems cut from brown cardstock, and a leaf cut from green paper to the white circle. Punch a ¼" hole at the top of the tag. Wrap red gingham ribbon around one side of the napkin holder. Thread the tag onto the ribbon; secure with a knot. Position a couple of foam dots behind the tag to hold it in place.

Cherry Recipe Box. Cut a piece of patterned paper to fit on the top of the recipe box and trim the corners with a corner rounder punch tool. Adhere the paper to the top of the box using an even coat of Mono Metal liquid glue. Cut two strips of patterned paper to the height of the box lid and adhere the strips around the lid, trimming off any excess. Center and wrap border stickers around the lid on top of the patterned paper, trimming off any excess. Cut two strips of patterned paper to the height of the box and trim the lengths as necessary so the papers cover the box. Apply strips of Wonder Tape to the backs of the two pieces around the outer edges. Working with one piece at a time, cover

the remaining paper area on the back with an even coat of Mono Metal liquid glue, and then wrap the paper around the box. Repeat with the second piece of patterned paper. (You may need to trim away some of the paper around the box's hinge.) If desired, cover the paper with one or more coats of Mod Podge to protect it from the wear of daily use. Adhere a piece of patterned paper behind the nameplate and stamp "Recipes" inside the window. Mark the holes for the nameplate on the front of the lid. Punch holes at the marked points with the Crop-A-Dile tool and then attach the nameplate with brads. Adhere two buttons, two cherry stems cut from brown cardstock, and a leaf cut from green paper to the front of the box.

Page 16
GIRL'S JEWELRY BOX

Materials

6" wide x 4" deep x 2" tall wooden box

Patterned paper: Crate Paper – Twirl Collection (Baby Doll, Tricycle, Girly Girl, and Dress Up)

Chipboard frame, Meadow acrylic paint, pink flower, crystal brad, pink ribbon, and rickrack trim: Making Memories

Small pink flowers: Jolee's By You

Self-adhesive gemstones: Hero Arts

Liquid craft glue

Mini double-sided adhesive glue dots: Glue Dots International

Other: foam brush, self-healing cutting mat, X-Acto knife

How to:

Paint the wooden box inside and out; set aside to dry. Cut the green paper to fit on the top of the box lid and adhere in place with liquid glue. Cut two ¾"-wide strips from the pink floral paper, apply a thin layer of glue to the back of one strip at a time, and adhere the strips to the bottom half of the box as shown. Trim away any excess paper. Apply glue to the chipboard frame and cover with the solid pink paper; let dry. Using an X-Acto knife and cutting mat, trim away the excess paper. Trim the striped paper slightly larger than the frame

49

opening and adhere to the back of the frame with glue dots. Pierce the rhinestone brad through the center of the pink flower and open the brad flat. Adhere the flower to the center of the framed paper with glue dots. Embellish the frame with self adhesive gemstones. Cut one piece of ribbon and two pieces of trim to 3" each. Adhere ribbon and trim to the box top in the upper-left corner. Using glue dots, adhere the embellished frame at an angle to the top of the box, covering the ends of the ribbon on the right side. Finish by attaching a small pink flower along each piece of ribbon and trim with glue dots.

Page 17
FLOWER MOBILE
Materials

Wire mobile with photo clips: Kikkerland

10 wooden flower shapes

Patterned paper: Crate Paper–Twirl Collection (Baby Doll, Tricycle, Girly Girl, and Dress Up)

Acrylic paint: Making Memories–Meadow

Self-adhesive vintage buttons: EK Success–The Attic by Rebecca Sower

Self-adhesive gemstones: Hero Arts

Liquid craft glue

Other: foam brush

How to:

Using the foam brush, paint all sides of the wooden flowers and set them aside to dry. Trace each flower shape twice onto the desired patterned paper and cut out just inside the marked lines. (This allows the paint on the wooden flowers to show around the edges.) Adhere a paper flower to each side of a painted flower using liquid glue. Embellish the flowers with self-adhesive gems and buttons. Clip each of the finished wooden flowers onto the wire mobile.

Page 19
PLANNER, COUPON, AND ADDRESS BOOKS: PLANNER

Materials

Patterned paper: Foof-A-La–Picadilly; Daisy D's–Carte Postale

Cardstock: 17 cream speckled sheets and 29 black sheets

Six 4¾" x 6½" envelopes

Chipboard

Jumbo pewter bookplate with brads: BasicGrey

Buttons

Ribbons (black ruffle, red silk, and gingham): May Arts

Inkpad: Clearsnap–Ancient Page Coal Black Dye

Small binder clips

Clear photo corners: Canson

Marker: EK Success–Zig Millennium (.01 mm tip) black

Computer, photo editing software, and printer

Calendar template: thedigichick.com–Marsha Zepeda (see "Resources" on page 63)

Double-sided adhesive tape: 3M–Scotch ATG 714 adhesive and dispenser

Hot glue gun and glue sticks

Quick-dry tacky glue: 3M–Scotch Quick-Dry Tacky Adhesive

Hole punch and hammer: Making Memories

Tab die and die-cutting tool: QuicKutz–Tab Die Set #QKDS-11 and Squeeze Die-Cutting hand tool

Other: ¼" hole punch, sewing machine and sewing thread

How to:

From the chipboard, cut two 8⅛" x 8¼" pieces and two ⅝" x 8⅛" strips. From the Picadilly paper, cut two 9¼" squares and one ⅝" x 8⅛" strip. From the Carte Postale paper, cut one 1½" x 9¼" strip and one ⅝" x 8⅛" strip. From the black cardstock, cut 25, pieces, 8" x 8½" and two pieces, 8" x 8¾". Center and adhere a large chipboard piece to the back of a Picadilly square using double-sided tape. Trim the paper diagonally at the corners. Fold the paper flaps over the cover and secure with tape. Repeat for the back cover.

Adhere the 1½" x 9¼" Carte Postale strip to the left edge of the front cover, wrapping the ends to the inside. Trace the inside of the bookplate onto the cream cardstock to make the label. In pencil write "Planner" and trace with the marker. Trim the label. Adhere the label to the front cover. Setting

the bookplate over the label, mark the holes. Punch the holes using the hole punch and a hammer. Attach the bookplate with brads. Distress cover edges by rubbing with the inkpad.

Adhere black ribbon over the seam between the front cover papers, wrap the ends to the inside, and secure with hot glue. Center the red ribbon over the black one and glue the ends only to the inside.

Score the 8" x 8¾" pieces of black cardstock, ¾" from the left edges (8" edges) and set aside. Adhere the Carte Postale strip to a chipboard strip to create the spine. Adhere the spine to the left edge of the scored black cardstock, centering it over the length and aligning the left edges. Apply double-sided tape to the back of the front cover, about ¼" from all edges and about every inch horizontally and vertically.

With the spine facing up, center the front cover and place it, patterned side up, over the black cardstock so that there is about ⅛" gap between the spine and the cover. (The cover is larger than the black cardstock, so be sure to allow equal space at the top and bottom.) Repeat for the back cover, except adhere the Picadilly strip to the cardstock strip for the back spine.

Stack the 25 pieces of black cardstock so that the paper is 8½" wide by 8" high. Score each piece of the black cardstock ¾" from the left edge. Trim a shallow arc 4½" long and centered along the right edge of 12 sheets of paper for the pocket fronts. (Use the first one as a template for cutting the others.) Stack the papers alternating plain papers with ones that have the arcs cut out. Use a tiny bit of tape to attach the corners of each pair of papers to create 12 pocket pages. There will be one page left over. Zigzag stitch around three sides of each pocket, leaving the side with the arc open, and staying 1/16" from away from the score line on the opposite side. Tie off the thread ends on the back sides. Stitch the remaining page on all sides staying 1/16" away from the score line. This page will be the first page in the planner.

Punch ¼" holes in the spine, 2" from the top and 2" from the bottom. Use the front cover as a template to mark the holes for the back and the pocket pages. Punch the holes. Assemble the album pages inside the covers. Thread lengths of gingham and ruffled ribbon through each of the holes and knot together.

Stack two buttons of different sizes and secure with glue. Glue the buttons over the red ribbon near the upper edge of the front cover.

50

Using the die-cutting tool, cut 24 tabs from the Picadilly paper, 12 tabs from black cardstock (for stability), 12 tab labels from the cream cardstock, and then write the months on each label. Adhere a Picadilly tab to both sides of each black tab, adhere a cream label to each tab, and secure the tabs to the pocket pages. Download the calendar templates from digichick.com. Using your favorite photo-editing program, open the calendar templates and size to 5¾" wide by 6" high. Print out the calendar pages on the cream cardstock and trim close to the edges. Use clear photo corners to attach a calendar page to the front of each pocket.

Cut 12 tag shapes from cream cardstock to fit in the pockets. Sew ribbons to the top edge of half and glue buttons to the rest. Tuck the tags into the pockets. Write "Receipts" and the months onto six envelopes and clip the envelopes to every other page with the binder clips.

Page 19
PLANNER, COUPON, AND ADDRESS BOOKS: COUPON BOOK
Materials

4" x 6" photo album: Pioneer

Patterned paper: Foof-A-La–Picadilly; 7 Gypsies–1936

Cardstock: cream speckled and black

Inkpad: Clearsnap–Colorbox Fluid Chalk Chestnut Roan

Black ribbon

Marker: EK Success–Zig Millennium (.01 mm tip) black

Double-sided adhesive tape: 3M–Scotch ATG 714 adhesive and dispenser

Hot glue gun and glue sticks

Quick-dry tacky glue: 3M–Scotch Quick-Dry Tacky Adhesive

Tab die and die-cutting tool: QuicKutz–Tab Die Set #QKDS-11 and Squeeze Die-Cutting hand tool

How to:

Cut two rectangles of the Picadilly paper, 2" larger than the front album cover. Cut one rectangle of paper equal to the width of the album spine and 1¼" longer. Apply double-sided tape along the front edges of the album and several strips of tape running from top to bottom. Center the album front on the wrong side of one of the large paper rectangles. Trim the outside corners of the paper at an angle. Repeat for the back. Apply adhesive to the spine and wrap the excess paper onto the spine.

Center and adhere the paper for the spine to the album. Trim the edges of the papers to fit as desired when the flaps are folded to the inside. Adhere the paper edges to the inside with hot glue.

Cut two rectangles from black cardstock to cover the inside front and back covers; adhere in place. Using hot glue, adhere a ribbon to each side of the spine, over the paper seam, and continue adhering the ribbon from the outside to the inside to make a complete loop around the book. Die cut eight tabs from black cardstock and eight tab labels from cream cardstock using the QuicKutz tool and the tab die. Adhere the labels to the die cut tabs with tacky glue. Write categories on the labels and adhere the tabs to the book pages. Cut letter rectangles out of 7 Gypsies paper to spell "coupons," and distress the edges by rubbing with the inkpad. Adhere the letters to the book front with tacky glue, overlapping to fit.

Page 19
PLANNER, COUPON, AND ADDRESS BOOKS: ADDRESS BOOK

Materials

Patterned paper: Foof-A-La–Picadilly, Daisy D's–Carte Postale, 7 Gypsies–1936

Cream cardstock

Chipboard

Inkpad: Clearsnap–Colorbox Fluid Chalk Chestnut Roan

Label stamp: Paper Salon–Monogram Builder

Clear acrylic stamp block

Computer and word processing program for inside pages (QuarkXPress was used here)

Marker: EK Success–Zig Millennium (.01 mm) tip black

Double-sided adhesive tape: 3M–Scotch ATG 714 adhesive and dispenser

Quick-dry tacky glue: 3M–Scotch Quick-Dry Tacky Adhesive

Tab die and die-cutting tool: QuicKutz–Tabs and Squeeze Die-Cutting hand tool

Access to a professional photocopy center for the binding

How to:

Cut *each* of two pieces of chipboard, one piece of Carte Postale paper, one piece of Picadilly, and two pieces of 1936 paper to 5½" x 8¼". Cut a 4¼" square from Picadilly, rip it diagonally, and distress all the edges by rubbing them with the inkpad.

Adhere the Carte Postale paper to a piece of chipboard using double-sided tape to make the front cover. Adhere the ripped triangle of paper to the lower-right corner. Stamp a label onto cream cardstock and write the word "addresses" on the label. Adhere the label to the book. Adhere one piece of the 1936 paper to the inside front cover, making sure the alphabet is positioned correctly. Adhere one piece of 1936 paper to the remaining chipboard piece, flip over, and adhere the remaining piece of Picadilly paper.

Design the inside address pages on a word processing program, fitting two address pages per sheet of paper. (Be sure to format the page so when trimmed, the address pages will have adequate space on the left edge to allow for binding.) Print the address pages and trim to size.

Using the QuicKutz hand tool, die cut nine tabs each from the Picadilly paper and black cardstock and nine labels from cream cardstock. Using tacky glue, adhere the Picadilly tabs to the black tabs, and then adhere the tab labels. Print letters on the labels. Adhere the tabs to the edges of the pages. Take the completed address book to a photocopy center to have spiral bound.

Page 20
SEASIDE FRAMES: "OCEAN" FRAME

Materials

9" x 11" wooden frame: DecoArt

Patterned papers: Scenic Route; Fancy Pants Designs; Paper Wishes

Chipboard letters: BasicGrey

Acrylic paint (Manila), chipboard flourish, and metal brads: Making Memories

Inkpad: Clearsnap–ColorBox Fluid Chalk Chestnut Roan

Personal photo to fit frame opening

White craft glue: Aleene's Original Tacky Glue

Double-sided tape: Suze Weinberg's Wonder Tape

Crop-A-Dile Eyelet and Snap Punch: We R Memory Makers

Other: paintbrush and wire cutters

How to:

Paint the wood frame, leaving areas of the wood exposed. Cut four different 2" squares from the patterned papers. Cut each square once diagonally to make the corner triangles. Cut patterned paper into 2"-wide strips, and then cut each strip into smaller segments. Arrange the paper pieces over the frame front and trim as needed. Brush paint around the edges of each paper and let dry. Glue the papers to the frame front. Paint the chipboard letters and flourish, and adhere paper to two of the letters. Rub the inkpad around the edges of the letters and flourish for a distressed look. Trim 1/8" from each of the metal brad prongs with wire snips. Punch holes through the chipboard pieces with the Crop-A-Dial tool, and install the brads. Attach the chipboard pieces to the frame with double-sided tape. Insert a personal photo in the frame opening.

Page 20
SEASIDE FRAMES: WAVE AND BUTTON FRAMES

Materials (for two frames)

2 wooden frames (5" x 5")

Patterned papers: Scenic Route; Fancy Pants Designs; Paper Wishes

Chipboard number: Li'l Davis Designs

Chipboard letters: Making Memories

Chipboard corners

Black acrylic paint

Assorted buttons

Kraft raffia

2 personel photos to fit frame openings

White craft glue: Aleene's Original Tacky Glue

Crop-A-Dile Eyelet and Snap Punch: We R Memory Makers

Other: paintbrush

How to:

Cut and adhere patterned paper to the front of each frame.

Button Frame. Cover a chipboard corner with patterned paper and adhere it to the frame. Adhere buttons to the remainder of the frame. Punch a hole on the right and left side of the chipboard number and thread and knot raffia through each hole. Adhere the number on top of the buttons in the lower-left corner of the frame. Insert a personel photo in the frame opening.

Wave Frame. Cut a series of wave shapes in a 1⅜" strip of patterned paper. Adhere the wave strip to the lower edge of the frame. Paint the chipboard letters black, let dry, and adhere to the frame. Tear a corner from patterned paper and adhere it to the upper-left corner of the frame. Insert a personal photo in the frame opening.

Page 22
PINK ORGANIZERS

Materials (for one file box, one binder, and one expandable file)

11¾" wide x 9¼" deep x 10¾" tall pink metal bin with attached lid

10" x 11¾" black fabric-bound three-ring binder

4½" x 9¾" expandable file: Smead–70636

Patterned paper: Me and My Big Ideas; Scrapworks–Formal Affair English Ivy

Cardstock: white and black; Color Mates–Dark Fairytale Pink

Chipboard

Label sticker: Making Memories

Acrylic paint: Delta Ceramcoat–Peony; DecoArt–Americana Lamp (Ebony) Black

Rub-ons: Hambly Screen Prints–Vintage Motifs

Self-adhesive pink gemstone oval frames: Heidi Swapp–Bling

Crystal stickers: Mark Richards

Crystal Brads: Making Memories

Rhinestone flower button and flat button

¼" eyelet

Ribbons (polka-dot, velvet, and gingham)

¼"-wide elastic

Black thread

Marker: EK Success–Zig Millennium (.01 mm tip) black

Template: large label (page 62)

Double-sided adhesive tape: 3M–Scotch ATG 714 adhesive and dispenser

Hot glue gun and glue sticks

Quick-dry tacky glue: 3M–Scotch Quick-Dry Tacky Adhesive

Liquid glue: US ArtQuest–Perfect Paper Adhesive

Scrapbook paper piercer: Making Memories

Tab die and die-cutting tool: QuicKutz–Tabs and Squeeze Die-Cutting hand tool

Other: ¼" hole punch, detail paintbrush, foam brush, hand-sewing needle, sandpaper, scoring tool, wire cutters

How to:

Everything Binder. Cut two 8½" x 11¾" rectangles and two 10" x 11¾" rectangles from the large-print paper. Using Peony paint and a dry foam brush, paint the paper, making sure the pattern shows through; let dry. Adhere the two small papers to the binder front and back using double-sided tape. Attach the large paper pieces to the inside front and back covers in the same manner. Sand the edges to round the corners. Using a dry foam brush, apply black paint to the edges of the binder and onto the edges of the cover papers. Trace the large label template on page 62 onto white cardstock and cut it out. Apply black paint with a dry foam brush to the edges of the label and let dry. Adhere the label to the binder and add the gemstone frame. Inside the oval write a title.

Lay the large polka-dot ribbon face up. Cut two pieces of gingham ribbon 6" long and fold each in half around the polka-dot ribbon so that the ends of the ribbons stick out to the right. Use a paper piercer to pierce a hole in each of the folded ribbons just outside of the polka-dot ribbon and secure with a small crystal brad. Follow the same instructions to add a pink velvet ribbon between the gingham ones, with the ends pointing the other direction. Lay the polka-dot ribbon over the front of the binder and adjust the spacing of the three ribbons. Be sure there is enough polka-dot ribbon above the embellishments to wrap to the inside cover. Adhere the top edge of the polka-dot ribbon to the inside of the binder with hot glue and glue the rest of the ribbon over the edges of the papers on the front, keeping the ribbon embellishments in the desired position. Adhere the bottom end of the ribbon to the inside cover.

Paint any uncovered portion near the three-ring mechanism of the inside binder black. Cut eight 8¾" x 11¼" rectangles from pink cardstock. Cut one 8¾" x 4½" rectangle from the small print paper. Using a dry foam brush, paint the edges of the paper. Run a line of double-sided adhesive tape along three edges of the paper to create a pocket. Adhere it to the bottom edge of one of the cardstock papers. Die cut seven tabs from black cardstock and seven tab labels from white cardstock using the QuicKutz hand tool and tab die. Adhere the labels to the tabs with tacky glue and let dry. Write titles on the labels and adhere the tabs to the seven remaining pieces of cardstock. Punch holes in the left edge of all eight papers and insert the pages into the binder as page dividers.

Expandable Bill File. Paint the large print paper with Peony paint using a dry foam brush, making sure the pattern shows through; let dry. Cut one 4½" x 9¾" rectangle from the painted paper for the inside front and one 9⁹⁄₁₆" x 9¾" rectangle for the front flap which will fold to cover the back. Cut one 4½" x 9⁹⁄₁₆" rectangle to cover the inside flap and go down into the inside back. Adhere the cut pieces to the file with double-sided tape. Round the corners of the front flap. Using a dry foam paintbrush and black paint, paint the edges of the paper around the file. Punch a ¼" hole in the lower center of the flap and install an eyelet in the hole. Thread the ends of a 13" length of black elastic through the hole and stitch the ends together. Stitch a button over the ends to cover the stitching. The button will prevent the elastic from being pulled through the eyelet.

Die cut 12 tabs from black cardstock and 12 tab labels from white cardstock using the QuicKuts hand tool and tab die. Adhere the labels to the tabs with tacky glue, let dry, and write numbers on the labels. Attach a tab to each divider.

Write "Bills" onto the label sticker. Using a foam brush, lightly brush black paint on the edges of the label and let dry. Adhere the label sticker to the file. Attach crystal stickers to the outer edges of the flap.

File Box. Paint the large-print paper with Peony paint using a dry foam brush, making sure the pattern shows through. Cut paper to fit each side of the bin, cutting the front and back pieces ½" longer to allow for wrapping around the corners. Measure and then cut a slit to fit around the latch closure. Using Perfect Paper Adhesive, adhere the front paper to the bin first, then the back paper, and then the side pieces.

Adhere ribbon around the upper and lower edges of the paper using a glue gun. Cut a white oval from cardstock to match the oval gemstone frame. Add the small Hambly rub-on to the center. With a dry foam brush, apply Peony paint around the edge of the white oval and let dry. Adhere the oval to the bin and add the gemstone frame. Adhere a rhinestone button to the rub-on image with hot glue. Add a rub-on to the upper-left side of the lid. Remove the prongs from a large pink crystal brad and three small brads using wire cutters. Attach the large brad to the rub-on and the small brads to the front of the bin above the latch with hot glue.

Tie ribbons to the handle and trim the ends. Using black paint and a detail brush, paint a double-line border on the latch closure, following the outline of the latch.

To create the file folders, cut 14 pieces of pink cardstock to fit in the bin. Score each piece ½" from one long edge. Apply double-sided adhesive tape to one cardstock piece along the scored edge and attach the scored edge of a second piece of cardstock to the adhesive. (This will create a folder with a flat bottom.) Follow the same procedure to create the remaining folders. Die cut seven file tabs from black cardstock and seven tab labels from white cardstock using the QuicKutz hand tool and tab die. Using Perfect Paper Adhesive, attach the labels to the tabs and attach the tabs the folders. Handwrite the file names onto the labels.

Page 24
THREE-RING RECIPE BINDER
Materials

8½" x 11" D-ring binder: American Crafts–Modern Album

Patterned paper: Flair Designs–Farmer's Market and Picnic Table

Chipboard

Acrylic paint (Shopping Bag) and chipboard frame: Making Memories

Alphabet stamps: KI Memories–Newsprint Lower Alphas

Inkpads: Tsukineko–VersaColor Evergreen; Clearsnap–Colorbox Fluid Chalk Chestnut Roan

Ribbon and rickrack: May Arts

Jute twine

Double-stick tape: Suze Weinberg's Wonder Tape

Decoupage medium: Plaid–Matte Mod Podge

Crop-A-Dile Eyelet and Snap Punch: We R Memory Makers

Other: foam brush and paintbrush

How to:
Cut patterned paper to fit on the chipboard portion of the album cover; brush Mod Podge over the inside back binder cover and adhere the paper to the binder. Let dry, and then trim around the corners. Repeat for the back and front covers. Wrap two ribbons and a piece of rickrack around the front cover; secure the ends to the back side. Adhere paper to the inside front cover, covering the ribbon ends. If desired, coat papered sections with Mod Podge to protect from the wear of everyday use. Cut two labels from paper, adhere to chipboard with Mod Podge, and let dry. Cut out the labels and punch two holes in the lower-right corner of one using the Crop-A-Dile tool. If desired, coat with Mod Podge and let dry. Thread ribbon and twine through the holes and knot. Adhere labels to the cover with double-stick tape. Paint the chipboard frame and let dry. Rub the edges with the Chestnut Roan inkpad for a distressed look. Adhere the frame on top of a piece of scrap gingham paper and stamp "eat." in the opening. Punch a hole at the top and bottom of the frame with the Crop-A-Dile tool, thread and knot ribbon through each hole, and then adhere the frame to the cover.

Page 24
COFFEE CLOCK

Materials
13"-diameter clock

Patterned paper: Flair Designs–Coffee Talk; Daisy D's–Red Polka Dot; Martha Stewart Crafts–Sycamore Bark Crosshatch

Acrylic paint (Chocolate and Red Wagon), circle rims for tag maker tool, and Mailbox Alphabet: Making Memories

Chipboard numbers: BasicGrey; Li 'l Davis Designs

Stickers: Mrs. Grossman's – Pen & Ink Coffee

Decoupage medium: Plaid – Matte Mod Podge

Mini double-sided adhesive glue dots: Glue Dots International

Tag maker tool: Making Memories

Other: foam brush, paintbrush, sandpaper

How to:

Carefully remove the clock hardware and hands. Cut a piece of Sycamore Bark paper to fit the clock face. Brush an even coat of Mod Podge over the face of the clock, cover the face with the paper circle, and let dry. Unevenly brush a coat of brown paint over the patterned paper, leaving parts of the paper showing. Cut an 11¾" circle from red polka-dot paper and an 11" circle from coffee-patterned paper. Brush brown paint around the edge of the smaller circle and let dry. Glue the two paper circles to the center of the clock face, cutting a hole through the centers to accommodate the clock hardware. Lightly sand the rims of four metal circle tags, and then cover them with a coat of red paint. Cut circles from patterned paper to fit inside the rims, position the paper inside the rims, and then pinch the rims closed using the tag maker tool. Position a sticker in the center of each tag. Cover chipboard numbers with two coats of brown paint and let dry. Arrange and adhere the tags and numbers to the clock face with glue dots. Spell "JAVA" across the center of the face using the self-adhesive Mailbox Alphabet letters. Reassemble the clock's hardware.

Page 25
DESK AND SUPPLY ORGANIZERS
Materials List

Desk organizer: Creative Imaginations – Bare Elements Gabriel

Supply organizer: Creative Imaginations – Bare Elements Yvonnie

Patterned paper: BasicGrey – Blush Collection (Tease and Boyfriend); Making Memories – Boho Chic Collection, Lauren pack (Box Flower)

Spray paint: Rust-Oleum – Brown Hammered

Flowers: Daisy D's Paper Co. – Fresh Fabric Flowers

Self-adhesive rhinestones: K & Company – Peppermint Twist by Brenda Walton

Brads: Making Memories – Antique Copper Mini Circle

Letters: DCWV – Rockstar Metal Rustic Alphabet

Ribbon

Turquoise stamp pad

2 sepia-colored personal photos

Glue gun and glue sticks

Spray adhesive: Krylon

Other: sponge, tape, newspaper

How to:

Mask the desk organizer with the newspaper, leaving the base and frames exposed. Mask the units of the supply organizer, leaving the base and the tops of each container exposed. Following manufacturer's instructions, apply two layers of spray paint to the unmasked areas using even strokes. Let dry and remove the newspaper.

Cut the patterned papers to fit the surfaces of the desk organizer and to fit around each container of the supply organizer. Adhere the paper pieces to the corresponding surfaces. Adhere ribbon to the edges of some sections as shown.

Adhere the letters to the supply organizer containers to spell one word on each container: "pencils," "pens," "etc," and "etc." Adhere letters to the desk organizer to spell "girlz" in the center frame. Insert brads through the centers of some flowers and adhere rhinestones to the centers of some. Adhere the flowers to the organizers using the glue gun. Using a sponge, rub some color from the stamp pad onto the exposed white edges of the desk organizer. Insert personal photos into the remaining two photo frames on the desk organizer front. Set the supply organizer containers on the base.

Page 26
KEY HOOK AND PHOTO DISPLAY

Materials

White key hook and photo display

Patterned paper: Crate Paper Brunch Collection – Conversation, Sky, RSVP, Linen

Chipboard scrolls, metal photo corner, pinked-edge chipboard circle frame, self-adhesive metal molding: Making Memories

Alphabet stickers: Creative Imaginations

4" x 6" personal photo

Liquid craft glue

Mini double-sided adhesive glue dots: Glue Dots International

Other: foam brush, self-healing cutting mat, X-Acto knife

How to:

Cut and adhere striped paper pieces to the key hook and photo display. Cut the molding strips to fit across the upper and lower edges of the striped border and adhere in place. Adhere paper (solid side up) to the chipboard circle and scrolls, let dry, and then trim using an X-Acto knife and cutting mat. Cut a circle shape from the RSVP patterned paper a little larger than the opening of the chipboard frame and adhere to the circle so the solid side shows inside the frame. Cut a small trapezoid from patterned paper and adhere to the center of the circle. Adhere the metal photo corner with glue dots at the top of the trapezoid to create a "house" in the circle. Adhere the scrolls and the circle to the key hook and photo display. Cut a piece of paper (solid side up) to fit in one frame opening and use stickers to spell "home sweet home". Insert the message and the photo into the picture openings.

Page 27
WELCOME PHOTO TRAY

Materials

11" x 14" unfinished wooden tray

Patterned paper: Crate Paper Brunch Collection – RSVP, Sky, Lantern, Conversation, Canopy, Linen

Chipboard letters, chipboard scroll, chipboard scalloped photo corners: Making Memories

White craft paint

Red silk flower

Buttons: Foof-A-La

4" x 6" personal photograph

Decoupage medium: Plaid – Matte Mod Podge

Liquid craft glue

Mini double-sided adhesive glue dots: Glue Dots International

Other: foam brush, self-healing cutting mat, X-Acto knife, wall hanging hardware

How to:

Paint the tray and let dry. Cut six 1⅝" x 2⅛" pieces from each of the six patterned papers. Arrange the rectangles on the tray surface so there is one of each pattern in each row. Adhere the rectangles in place and let dry. Cover the scalloped photo corners with the solid side of the RSVP paper and cover the letters and scroll with the solid side of the Linen paper. Adhere the items to the tray. Mat the photo with a triple mat and adhere the photo to the tray. Adhere the silk flower to the tray, a button to the flower center, and three buttons to each of the photo corners with glue dots. Attach wall hanging hardware to the back of the tray.

Page 28
EMBELLISHED BULLETIN BOARD WITH COORDINATING TACKS
Materials

18" x 22" framed bulletin board

Patterned paper: blue; K & Company– Hopscotch Boy Toy Toss

Mixed font foam alphabet stamps: Charmed Enamel All Boy charms, and Jumbo Pebble Brads In Bloom: Making Memories

Red acrylic paint

Self-adhesive ribbon: KI Memories–Alpine Dottie

½" flat-head thumb tacks

Decoupage medium: Plaid–Matte Mod Podge

Superglue–Future Glue Gel

Other: ¾" circle punch, foam brush, wire cutters

How to:

Embellished Bulletin Board. Cut patterned paper into strips the width of the frame. If the pattern is specifically vertical or horizontal, make sure to cut strips so the pattern will be correctly oriented on the frame. Brush Mod Podge onto the flat surface of the frame and adhere the paper strips to it. To protect the surface of the paper, apply one or more layers of Mod Podge over the paper. Allow to dry. Apply self-adhesive ribbon around the inside bevel of the frame, trimming each end at an angle to create mitered corners. Stamp the words, "jump," "run," "play," and "laugh" on the cork surface of the board using foam stamps and red paint.

Coordinating Tacks. Use wire cutters to remove the prongs from the brads, taking care to secure the prongs and prevent them from flying about. Punch a ¾" circle from blue paper and adhere the truck charm to the front of it. Adhere the tacks to the backs of the snipped brads and metal charms with superglue.

Page 29
DECORATED PAPIER-MÂCHÉ LETTER "E"

Materials

12" papier-mâché letter

Patterned paper: K & Company– Hopscotch

White cardstock 2⅛" x 4¼" manila tag

Dimensional stickers: K & Company–Grand Adhesions Hopscotch

Ribbons (red, blue stripe, orange polka dot, and black-and-white gingham)

Red metal nameplate

Foam alphabet stamps: Making Memories–Mixed Font

Alphabet stamps: Stampendous–Small Typewriter Alphabet

Red acrylic paint Red inkpad

Black marker

Double-sided tape: Suze Weinberg's Wonder Tape

Decoupage medium: Plaid–Matte Mod Podge

Other: ¼" hole punch, ¾" circle punch, circle cutter, foam brush

How to:

Cut strips of blue paper to fit the depth of the letter and adhere the strips to the sides of the letter with Mod Podge. Cut various papers into strips equal to the width of the letter front. Arrange the strips on the front of the letter, cut and tear them to the desired lengths, and then adhere in place with Mod Podge. Cut a 3" circle from patterned paper. Cover the manila tag with patterned paper. Punch two ¾" circles from blue paper and adhere one to the top of the circle and one to the top of the tag. Punch a ¼" hole through each of the blue circles. Using red paint and foam alphabet stamps, stamp the child's name on the tag

and two asterisks and a partial asterisk on the circle. Let the paint dry, and then apply a dimensional sticker to the circle. Tie both tags to the letter with ribbon. Adhere white cardstock to the back of the nameplate. Stamp and write "You are loved" inside the nameplate. Tie ribbon to each side of the nameplate and adhere the nameplate to the front of the letter using tape. If the project will be displayed in a high-traffic area, you may want to protect the surface of the project and the embellishments with one or more layers of Mod Podge before assembling.

Page 30
TURNED TABLE LEG PHOTO DISPLAY
Materials

Vintage distressed, turned table leg, 23¼" high x 3½" wide at base

Wood pillar candle holder or other wood craft base, 6" diameter x 2½" tall

Patterned paper: My Mind's Eye–Brother's, Play, Cute, Girl, Love, Just Perfect Flowers

Inkpads: Clearsnap–ColorBox Fluid Chalk Chestnut Roan and Ancient Page Permanent Dye Chocolate

Buttons

White Cheeky Board Clips, decorative brads, and rhinestone brads: Making Memories

Ribbon: BasicGrey–Infuse

Stamp: Inkadinkado–Maison Frames by Brenda Walton; Studio G-VS4911

Marker: EK Success–Zig Writer Chocolate

Acrylic paint: DecoArt–Americana Burnt Umber; Plaid–Apple Barrel Valentine Pink

Antiquing medium: Plaid–FolkArt Antiquing Polish Brown

Flower die cut: Sizzix–Sizzlits Flower and Center

Wood screws

Templates: large flower, medium flower, and small flower (page 61)

Personal photos

Mini double-sided adhesive foam dots: Plaid–All Night Media Pop Dots

Mini double-sided adhesive glue dots: Glue Dots International

Die-cutting tool: Sizzix Sidekick

Other: ⅛" hole punch, drill and drill bit, paintbrush, sandpaper, screwdriver, rag

How to:

Using the screwdriver, make dents in the wood base, paint it Burnt Umber, and let dry. Paint it pink, let dry, and then sand off paint in some areas to distress the finish. Brush antiquing medium on the base and rub off with a dry rag. Attach the base to the table leg with screws, predrilling as necessary.

Cut two large, three medium, and three small flowers from patterned paper using the templates on page 61. Cut one flower from patterned paper using the Sizzlits flower die cut and cutting tool. Distress the edges by rubbing with the Chestnut Roan inkpad. Layer the large, medium, and small flowers and flower die cut to create two large flowers and one medium multi-layered flower. (Reserve one small flower for later use.) Punch a hole in the center of each layered flower and secure with a brad or a brad layered over a button. (The button used here had one large hole rather than two small holes.) Roll each petal around a pencil to create dimension.

Rub the clips with the Chestnut Roan inkpad, and then wipe off the excess ink. Tie ribbons around the turned leg and attach the clips. Adhere the flowers to the leg with glue dots. Mat the photos with patterned paper and clip to the leg.

Cut a tag shape from a solid-colored paper and distress the edges with the Chestnut Roan inkpad. Stamp the frame image with Chocolate ink on another solid paper and trim close to the image. Handwrite "Family" on the label and adhere to the tag with foam dots. Attach the small reserved flower to the tag with foam dots, attach a button to the center, and clip to the leg.

Page 31
MAGNET BOARD

Materials

Cabinet door with recessed center panel

Patterned paper: My Mind's Eye – Brother's, Play, Cute, Girl, Love, Baby Girl, Happy

Paper for photo frame template

5" x 7" sheets of galvanized flashing: Amerimax Home Products

20" x 30" foamcore board: Elmer's

Flower die cut: Sizzix – Sizzlits Flower and Center

Inkpad: Clearsnap – Colorbox Fluid Chalk Chestnut Roan

Buttons

Self-adhesive rhinestone gems and white alphabet rub-ons: Making Memories

¾" magnet buttons: ProMAG

1½" vintage metal candy mold

Ribbon

Painted wood tag: Chatterbox

Templates: large flower, medium flower, and small flower (page 61)

Personal photo

Double-sided adhesive foam dots: Plaid – All Night Media Pop Dots

Double-sided adhesive tape: 3M – Scotch ATG 714 adhesive and dispenser

Hot glue gun and glue sticks

Mini double-sided adhesive glue dots: Glue Dots International

Other: tin snips

How to:

Cut the foam board to fit into the recessed area of the cabinet door. Adhere the flashing sheets to the foamcore board using a grid of double-sided tape and trim the sheets as necessary with a tin snips. Adhere patterned paper to the flashing surface, piecing as necessary and taking care to match any pattern in the paper. Attach the paper-covered foamcore board to the recessed area of the cabinet door with hot glue.

Cut two large, four medium, and one small flower from patterned papers using the templates on page 61 (use the reverse side of some of the papers). Cut one flower from patterned paper using the Sizzlits flower die cut and die-cutting tool. Distress the petals by rubbing the edges with the Chestnut Roan inkpad. Layer the large, medium, and small flower cutouts and flower die cut to create two large and one medium multilayered flowers. Secure the layers with glue dots. Fill the candy mold with a generous amount of hot glue and then quickly set a foam dot into the glue. You may need to layer another foam dot on top so the foam dot is level with the back of the mold. Remove the backing from the foam dot and press the mold firmly onto the center of a large flower. Adhere a gem to the center of the candy mold. Adhere a button or layered buttons to the centers of the remaining flowers with glue

dots. Roll the petals of all flowers around a pencil to add dimension. Attach magnets to the back of the flowers with hot glue.

To make the scalloped photo frame template, draw a 5⅞" x 7¼" rectangle and make marks ⅞" from each corner and about 1⅜" apart along the drawn lines. Connect the marks to create a scalloped edge. Cut out. Trace the scalloped frame template onto patterned paper, cut out, and rub the edges with the inkpad. Mat a photo with a double border (distress the paper edges with the inkpad) and adhere to the scalloped frame. Spell the word "happy" on the wood tag using the rub-ons. Tie ribbon around the framed photo and knot through the tag securing the tag in place.

Page 33
STYLISH ORGANIZERS AND CHECKBOOK COVER

Materials (for one notebook, one "dates to remember" file folder, and one checkbook cover)

6¾" x 4¾" pocket file folder

7⅝" x 9⅝" composition notebook

Clear vinyl checkbook cover: Sunday International

Patterned paper: BasicGrey – Infuse Collection

Chipboard label, chipboard letters, chipboard brackets, and ribbon: BasicGrey

Chipboard flower: Heidi Swapp

Tag: Avery – Jewelry Tag

Brown-and-white gingham ribbon

Inkpads: Clearsnap – Colorbox Fluid Chalk Chestnut Roan and Olive Pastel

Marker: EK Success – Zig Millennium (.01 mm tip) black

Acrylic paint: Plaid – Apple Barrel Burnt Umber, Valentine Pink, and Leaf Green

Computer, printer, and word processing program (QuarkXPress was used here)

½" square of hook-and-loop tape: Velcro

Double-sided adhesive tape: 3M – Scotch ATG 714 adhesive and dispenser

Mini double-sided adhesive glue dots: Glue Dots International

Punch: McGill – File Tab

Other: foam brush and sandpaper

How to:

Notebook. Paint the chipboard letters and the edges of the composition notebook with Burnt Umber and let dry. Using a dry foam brush, edge each letter with pink paint. Paint the chipboard brackets with pink paint, let dry, and then rub the edges with the Chestnut Roan inkpad. Rough the edges with sandpaper. Cut two 7" x 9⅝" rectangles each from patterned paper. Adhere the papers to the front and back of the book, trimming excess at the corners. Adhere ribbon to the book front, covering the paper edge. Adhere the letters and brackets. Cut one ⅜" x 9⅝" strip from Lace paper. Rub the edges with the inkpad, and adhere the strip to the back cover near the spine. Distress the edges of the notebook by rubbing with the inkpad.

"Dates to Remember" File Folder. Paint the top edge of the file folder Burnt Umber and let dry. Adhere patterned paper to the inside and outside of the flap. Trim the edges to match the existing flap. Rub the flap edges with the Chestnut Roan inkpad, for a distressed look. Cut a contrasting 2" x 6¾" rectangle of paper, rub the edges with the inkpad, and adhere it along the top of the flap.

Mix Burnt Umber and Leaf Green paint and use to paint the chipboard label. Let dry. Rub the edges of the label with the inkpad and write "dates to remember" with the marker. Tie a piece of ribbon to each end and adhere the label to the flap. Cut two 4½" x 6¾" pieces of paper, rub the edges with the inkpad, and adhere the pieces to the file front and back. Attach a button to the center front flap with mini glue dots. Attach the hook and loop tape under the flap.

Using a word processing program, create pages for each month. These pages were made with the month at the top and lines underneath so that each month filled a 4¼" x 5½" area (you can set up four months to a page this way). Print the pages out and trim each month to size. Punch 12 file tabs using the tab punch. Write the months on each tab and adhere the file pages. Insert the pages into the folder.

Checkbook Cover. Cut patterned paper to size and adhere to the cardstock insert (included with the checkbook cover). Distress the edges by rubbing with the inkpad. Adhere the chipboard flower to the lower-right corner of the insert. Punch a ¾" circle from paper and rub the edge with the Olive Pastel inkpad. Punch two ⅛" holes in center of the circle. Write "checks" on the tag and attach it to the circle with

the gingham ribbon. Adhere the circle to the pink flower with mini glue dots. Slip the insert into the cover.

Page 34
SCRAPLIGHT
Materials

Scraplight: Creative Imaginations

Patterned paper and punch-out letters: BasicGrey – Mellow

12" x 12" clear vellum paper

Dark red acrylic paint

4 small personal photos

Dotted adhesive: EK Success – Dotto Dots Dispenser with adhesive glue spot dots

Other: paintbrush, hole punch

How to:

Cut a heart from floral paper measuring 6" wide x 9¾" tall. Brush red paint around the edges and let dry. Adhere the heart to the middle of the vellum. Mat two 2" x 3" photos with striped paper. Adhere the matted photos and two others on top of the heart. Spell "love" and "cherish" using punch-out letters and adhere one word vertically on each side of the heart. Disassemble the light following the manufacturer's instructions. Position the design between the two layers of the shade and punch holes along the bottom of the design that align with the holes of the shade. Reassemble the light.

Page 35
EMBELLISHED LAMPSHADE
Materials

Lampshade and lamp base

Rub-on letter: Twelve Timbers – Wall Writing

Chipboard flowers (5 large and 9 small): Maya Road

Patterned papers: BasicGrey – Mellow

Brown and rose ribbons: Offray

Olive polka-dot ribbon

Acrylic paint: Making Memories – Manila

Crop-A-Dile Eyelet and Snap Punch: We R Memory Makers

Other: foam brush and paintbrush

How to:

Apply the rub-on letter to the center front of the shade. Paint the small chipboard flowers and let dry. Ahere paper to one side of each large flower, let dry, and then apply paint to the edges of the large flowers. Punch two holes at the top of each large flower and one hole at the top of each

small flower using the Crop-A-Dile tool. Punch a hole at the top of the shade directly above the rub-on. Use a piece of ribbon to tie a small flower to the shade. Continue punching holes in the shade and adding flowers, alternating between two small flowers and a large one. You may need up to three small flowers in a row at the back of the lamp to fill the space. Tie a large flower around the lamp base.

Page 36
MAGAZINE HOLDER

Materials

Wooden magazine holder: IKEA

Patterned paper: Autumn Leaves – French Twist

White cardstock

Chipboard frame: BasicGrey

Lime green glitter: Doodlebug Design

Glitter letter stickers: Making Memories

Green acrylic paint

Ribbon

Double-sided adhesive foam dots: All Night Media Pop Dots

Double-sided adhesive tape: Suze Weinberg's Wonder Tape

Glue pen

White craft glue: Aleene's Original Tacky Glue

Crop-A-Dile Eyelet and Snap Punch: We R Memory Keepers

Other: paintbrush

How to:

Cut patterned papers to fit on each side of the holder and adhere with glue. Paint the chipboard frame and let dry. Cover the frame with glue using the glue pen and then sprinkle with glitter, tapping off the excess. Spell out the holder's contents on patterned paper using alphabet stickers, making sure the lettering fits inside the frame opening. Back the paper with white cardstock for extra strength. Position the frame over the letters, trace around the frame, and cut inside the marked lines. Adhere the label to the back of the frame.

Wrap ribbon around the magazine holder as shown and secure with double-sided tape. Punch a hole on the right and left side of the frame using the Crop-A-Dile tool, and then thread and knot a small piece of ribbon through each hole. Adhere the frame to the front (tall) panel of the holder with foam dots.

Page 37
KEEPSAKE BOX

Materials

5½" wide x 5⅜" deep x 5½" tall wooden box (the one shown had a weathered yellow finish)

Patterned paper and buttons: Autumn Leaves–French Twist

Self-adhesive gemstones

Chipboard letter: BasicGrey

Pink acrylic paint

Pink glitter: Doodlebug Design

Double-sided adhesive glue dots: Glue Dots International

White craft glue: Aleene's Original Tacky Glue

Other: paintbrush and X-Acto knife

How to:

Remove any hardware from the box, if possible. Cut patterned papers to fit on the desired surfaces of the box. Adhere the papers to the box with craft glue. If any hardware was removed, locate the holes and pierce the paper using an X-Acto knife or other tool. Reattach the hardware. Adhere buttons in a row around the sides of the lid using glue dots. Adhere a gemstone to the center of each button. Paint a chipboard letter pink and let dry. Apply glue to the letter front, sprinkle with glitter, and tap off excess. Adhere the letter to the box.

Page 38
"FAMILY" WORD DISPLAY

Materials

4" and 6" wooden letters

Patterned paper: My Mind's Eye–Bohemian

Inkpad: Clearsnap–Colorbox Fluid Chalk Chestnut Roan

Ribbons and rickrack

Self-adhesive gemstones

Personal photos

Spray adhesive

White craft glue

Other: ¼" hole punch

How to:

Turn patterned papers wrong sides up. Trace letters or portions of letters in reverse onto the papers and cut out. To layer more than one paper on a letter, tear the edge on the top paper layer so the white of the paper shows, and then rub the edge with the inkpad to soften the look. Adhere any lower paper layers to the letters first, and then adhere any remaining paper layers with spray adhesive. Cut your photographs into tags, mat them with patterned paper, punch holes in the tops, and add a ribbon tie to each. Adhere the photo tags to the letters with glue. Embellish the letters with gemstones and assorted ribbons, either glued onto or tied around the letters.

Page 39
KIDS' "TO DO" BOARD
Materials

11" x 21" frame with wood backboard

Patterned paper: My Mind's Eye–Kaleidoscope; BasicGrey

Computer, word processing program, and printer

Font: Minus

⅛" dowels

Sewing machine and sewing thread

Hand-held pruner: Fiskars

White craft glue

Other: ¼" hole punch, 1" circle punch, 1½" circle punch, drill and ⅛" drill bit

How to:

Disassemble the frame and remove and discard all but the frame and backboard. Adhere patterned paper to the backboard, piecing as necessary. Reframe the board. Print each child's name on patterned paper to fill a space 1¾" x 4¼" and trim to size. Mat each name with patterned paper and zigzag stitch around the border. Adhere the names to the left side of the board in evenly spaced rows, leaving space for a

row on the bottom to hang extra disks. Print tasks on patterned paper and punch out with a 1½" circle punch. Punch a hole at the top of each disk. Use the 1" circle to punch completion disks from paper and punch a hole at the top of each disk. Cut ⅛" dowels into ⅝" sections with the pruner. Drill ⅛" holes, 1½" apart, across each of the rows (test that the dowels fit snugly in the holes without glue). Insert dowel pieces into the holes. Hang the task disks for each child on the dowels in each row and hang the extra disks on the bottom row.

Page 40
SPICE BOTTLE STORAGE UNIT

Materials

10 spice bottles

Two-tiered stand or spice rack

Paint: DecoArt–Americana Burnt Umber

Patterned paper: BasicGrey–Urban Couture Lux and Damask

Cardstock: ivory

Label stamp: Paper Salon–Monogram Builder

Inkpad: Clearsnap–Colorbox Fluid Chalk Chestnut Roan

Pen: American Crafts–Slick Writer (fine tip) Chestnut

Decoupage medium; Plaid–Matte Mod Podge

Liquid glue: US ArtQuest–Perfect Paper Adhesive

Circle punch (size depends on diameter of the bottle lid; a 1⅜" punch was used here): EK Success

Other: Sandpaper

How to:

Paint the edges of the tiered stand with Burnt Umber acrylic paint and let dry. Using the tiered stand as a template, trace the sections of the stand onto the Lux paper; cut out. Adhere the paper pieces to the corresponding sections of the stand and let dry. Sand the edges of the paper lightly, and then distress the edges by rubbing them with the inkpad.

Cut 10 strips of Damask paper to fit around the center of the bottles and adhere in place. Cut 10 strips of Damask paper to fit around the sides of the bottle lids and punch 10 circles from Damask paper for the tops of the lids. Adhere the paper pieces to the lids. Stamp 10 labels onto ivory cardstock with Chestnut Roan ink. Cut out the labels and write a supply name on each. Adhere a label to the center band of each bottle. If desired, cover the paper with one or more coats of Mod Podge to protect it from the wear of daily use. Set the bottles on the stand.

Page 41
LAZY SUSAN CRAFT-SUPPLY CENTER
Materials

Wooden lazy Susan, 15" in diameter

Turned spindle

Metal buckets (4" high x 4½" diameter at top)

Spray paint: Rust-Oleum–Painter's Touch Espresso Satin

Paint: Plaid–FolkArt Christmas Red

Antiquing medium: Plaid–FolkArt Antiquing Polish

Patterned paper: Basic Grey–Urban Couture Brocade

Cardstock: Ivory

Stamps: Inkadinkado–Maison Frames by Brenda Walton; Studio G–VS4911

Stampendous–Mini Corners

Inkpads: Clearsnap–Colorbox Fluid Chalk Chestnut Roan; Ranger–Archival Ink Crimson

Metal clips: Making Memories–Cheeky Board Clips

½" magnet buttons: ProMAG

Pen: Martha Stewart Crafts–Sepia Fine-Tip (.5mm tip) Writing Pen

Double-sided adhesive tape: 3M–Scotch ATG 714 adhesive and dispenser

Other: cotton rag, newsprint, sandpaper, wood glue, foam brush

How to:

Following manufacturer's instructions, spray paint the lazy Susan and the spindle with Espresso and set them aside to dry. Paint over the brown spindle with Christmas Red paint using a foam brush and allowing some of the brown paint show through. Let dry, and then use a foam paintbrush to apply the antiquing glaze. Remove the antiquing glaze quickly with a dry rag. Attach the spindle to the center of the lazy Susan with wood glue.

Use tape to mark a point on a bucket rim at the top and align a second tape mark

at the bottom of the bucket. Lay the metal bucket on its side on a piece of newsprint, with the tape marks down. Roll the bucket as you trace along the top and bottom edges and continue until you reach the tape marks. Connect the top and bottom lines at each end using a ruler and pencil. Cut on the marked lines, and hold the pattern to the bucket to check accuracy. Make any adjustments as necessary for a tight fit and add ¼" overlap allowance at one short end to finish the pattern. Use the pattern created as a guide to cut Brocade paper to fit around the buckets. Piece the paper as necessary at the back of the buckets. Adhere the Brocade paper to the buckets using double-sided adhesive tape.

Stamp six label images onto ivory card-stock with Crimson ink. Write the supply titles on the labels. Embellish the labels with decorative stamps and Chestnut Roan ink. Cut out the labels. Attach the labels to the Cheeky Board Clips and secure to the bucket, by placing a magnet on the inside of each bucket behind each clip. Set the buckets on the lazy Susan.

Page 42
COUNTDOWN TO CHRISTMAS

Materials

12" x 12" frame: K & Company

Tin: Altoids

Patterned paper: BasicGrey–Dasher Eggnog, Dasher Snowfall Cranberry, and Blitzen Poinsettia; Flair Designs–Christmas Carol Music

Cardstock: Ivory

Oval label: Rhonna Farrer DigiKit– Old Stamps Huge Brushes Companion Kit (see Two Peas in a Bucket in "Resources" on page 63)

Chipboard

Chipboard numbers: Lil' Davis Designs

Paint: Plaid–FolkArt Christmas Red;

Delta–Ceramcoat Seminole Green

Antiquing medium: Plaid–FolkArt Antiquing Polish Brown

Scroll foam stamp: Heidi Swapp–Drama

Cheeky Board Clips, foam alphabet stamps (Simply Fab and Misunderstood sets), rhinestone brads, and tag: Making Memories

Inkpad: Clearsnap–Colorbox Fluid Chalk Chestnut Roan

Eyelets

Ribbon

Silk poinsettia

Buttons

Computer, photo editing program, and printer

Font: Creating Keepsakes–CK Elegant

Double-sided adhesive tape: 3M–Scotch ATG 714 adhesive and dispenser

Hot glue gun and glue sticks

Liquid glue: US Artquest–Perfect Paper Adhesive

Hole punch and eyelet setter: Making Memories

Other: cheesecloth, sandpaper, wire cutters

How to:

Adhere Eggnog paper to a 12" x 12" piece of chipboard. Cut a 3¾" x 12" rectangle of music paper, stamp the scroll with green paint on the left edge, stamp the "C" using the Simply Fab set with red paint, and the rest of the word "Christmas," using the Misunderstood set. Let dry, and then adhere the music strip to the bottom of the Eggnog paper. Cut a 7" square each from chipboard and Snowfall paper and adhere the paper to the chipboard; then cut a 3" square window from the center to create a frame. Rub the edges of the frame with the inkpad for a distressed look. Trim one piece of music paper to 3½" square and adhere it to the Eggnog background, approximately 3½" from the top edge and 4" from each side. Center and adhere the frame over the music paper. Cut a 2" x 9" rectangle each from chipboard and Blitzen Poinsettia and adhere the paper to the chipboard. Rip the left edge of the paper-covered chipboard and rub with the inkpad. Adhere the strip to the background as shown.

Punch two holes through the back of the project, 4½" from the top and 5½" from each side of the design. Clip the brad prongs off of two rhinestone brads using wire cutters. Use hot glue to apply them to the front of two board clips. To attach the board clips to the holes, thread narrow ribbon through the hole of a button, and then through a hole in the background, through the back hole of the board clip, and then back through the hole in the back-ground. Insert it back through the second

59

hole in the button and knot the ends. Use the same process to attach the second board clip. Clip the Lil' Davis numbers to the board clips to display the countdown days. You will need a set of numbers from "0" to "9", and two of the number "1", and two of the number "2".

Pull a narrow ribbon through the holes of a button and tie the "Merry" tag to it. Glue the button to the Poinsettia and glue the Poinsettia to the layout.

Paint a portion of the frame with red paint and let dry. Use sandpaper to rough up the paint. Apply antiquing polish to a piece of cheese cloth and rub onto frame. Rub off any excess with dry cheesecloth.

In your favorite photo-editing program, size the oval label from the Rhonna Farrer digital kit to 5⅜" wide by 3" high. Add "Countdown To" using the CK Elegant font in red. Print out onto ivory cardstock, adhere to chipboard, and trim along the oval shape. Punch holes in the oval chipboard and add eyelets as shown. Loop two pieces of ribbon through the eyelets and tie loosely to the frame so the "Countdown To" label hangs from the top of the frame. Insert the layout into the frame. You will not need the glass provided with the frame.

To decorate the Altoids tin cut paper to fit on all surfaces and adhere in place with Perfect Paper Adhesive. Sand the edges of the tin and paper and rub with the inkpad. In your favorite photo editing program, size the rectangle label from the Rhonna Farrer digital kit to 2¾" wide x 1¾" high, and add "Countdown Numbers" using the CK Elegant font in red. Print onto ivory cardstock, cut out, and adhere to the tin.

Page 43
"JOY" FRAMED

Materials

Oval frame with an 8" x 10" window opening

Patterned paper: BasicGrey–Fruitcake Collection Berry Branch/Marachino Cherry and Tidings/Wintermint

White cardstock

Chipboard letters (j, o, and y): BasicGrey–Undressed Chipboard Monograms

Chipboard

Postcard: Scanned image of a vintage 1912 postcard

Inkpad: Clearsnap–Colorbox Fluid Chalk Chestnut Roan

Scraps of felted wool: burgundy and green

Cotton floss: DMC–498 red and 937 green (optional)

Snowflake charm: Scrap Arts

Ribbons: 1½"-wide for hanger and three assorted narrow ribbons for embellishment

Templates: holly leaf and berry (page 62)

Computer, photo editing software, printer, and scanner

Double-sided adhesive tape: 3M–Scotch ATG 714 adhesive and dispenser

Hot glue gun and glue sticks

Mini double-sided adhesive glue dots: Glue Dots International

Liquid glue: US ArtQuest–Perfect Paper Adhesive

Other: sandpaper, small paintbrush

How to:

Remove the back and glass from the frame. Using the glass as a template, carefully trace the oval onto a piece of chipboard and cut out. Using the chipboard as a template, trace the oval onto the Berry Branch paper and cut out. Adhere the paper oval to the chipboard with double-sided tape. Trace the chipboard letters onto the Tidings paper, cut them out, and adhere them to the chipboard letters with Perfect Paper Adhesive; let dry. Sand the edges of the letters and rub with the inkpad for a distressed look. Place the Berry Branch oval back into the frame. Adhere the letters to the background to spell "joy". Scan a postcard and resize it in your favorite photo editing program to 2⅛" wide x 1½" high. Print the postcard onto white cardstock, trim to size, and then rough up the edges with sandpaper. Rub the edges with the inkpad. Adhere it to the lower portion of the letter "j" with mini glue dots and attach the snowflake. Tie a knot in each of three ribbons and trim the ends. Using hot glue, attach the knots to the left side of the letter "o". Trace the holly leaf and berry templates onto felted wool and cut out. Use floss to stitch details onto the holly and berries, if desired. Hot glue them to the letter "y". Hot glue two pieces of wide ribbon to the back of the frame and tie in a bow.

CRAFT-SUPPLY BOX AND PAINTBRUSH HOLDER

Materials (for one box and one paintbrush holder)

7¾" x 11¼" x 4¼" photo storage box

Cylindrical container, about 8½" tall with a 4" diameter (this one contained large cookie wafers)

Patterned paper: K & Company

Self-adhesive gemstones

Ribbon, rickrack, and other trim

Computer, word processing program and printer

Font: Hurricane

White craft glue

Other: sandpaper

How to:

Craft-Supply Box. Cut and adhere patterned paper to the top and sides of the box lid and to the sides of the box. Adhere a piece of narrow rickrack around the sides of the lid near the lower edge using glue. Print a craft-supply title on patterned paper and cut a rectangle from the paper for the lid label, centering the title. Mat the title with patterned paper. Make a smaller label for the end of the box and apply gemstones under the title. Adhere a strip of rickrack under title on the lid label and apply gemstones along the sides of the rickrack in the recesses. Also apply gemstones around the perimeter of the box lid, spacing about 1¼" apart. Adhere the labels to the box.

Paintbrush Holder. Divide the circumference of the container by four and cut four strips of assorted papers to this width by the height of the container. Lightly sand all pieces for a slightly distressed look. Adhere the strips to the side of the container with glue. Print a craft-supply title on patterned paper and cut a rectangle from the paper for the label, centering the title. Mat the title with patterned paper and adhere to the container. Adhere trim to the top and bottom edges of the container. Embellish both the upper edge of the container and the label with gemstones.

Templates

Large flower

Small flower

Bird

Branch

Medium flower

Large label

Berry
Cut 3.

Holly leaf
Cut 2.

Scroll

Fold line

Leaf

TEMPLATES

Resources

American Crafts

www.americancrafts.com

(chipboard three-ring album – Modern Album)

Creative Imaginations

www.cigift.com

(scraplight)

IKEA

www.ikea.com

(mini chest of drawers and magazine file)

Kikkerland

www.kikkerland.com

(wire mobile with photo clips)

Storables

www.storables.com

(jewelry box)

The Vintage Workshop

www.thevintageworkshop.com

(cowboy image)

The DigiChick

www.thedigichick.com

(calendar template)

Two Peas In a Bucket

www.twopeasinabucket.com

(DigiKit: Rhonna Farrer – Old Stamps Huge Brushes Companion Kit)

About the Designers

Saralyn Ewald is a freelance designer based out of Portland, Oregon. Having grown up with handmade doll clothes and paper box dollhouses, she credits her mom for her crafting roots. Today, her "I can make that!" attitude keeps her sketchbook brimming with ideas and her worktable constantly messy. Saralyn has contributed to several other Martingale & Company titles.

Christine Falk has enjoyed crafts and home decorating for much of her adult life. She has had several designs published in books over the last few years. Her most recent project designs can be found in *Scrapbooking Off the Page...and on the Wall* (Martingale & Company, 2006).

Gina Hamann has been scrapbooking and doing other paper projects for over nine years. She is passionate about doing projects for her family and loved ones. She says, "I begin with the words that I want them to hear and build a project around them."

Nicole Johnson has enjoyed many years in a creative-design career, first as an interior designer; then later as a creative designer at Archiver's. She has since decided to continue that love, yet also fulfill her desire to be a stay-at-home mom in Burnsville, Minnesota, by working from home as a designer. She and her husband, Tim, have three children. Regarding her talent, she says, "I have been crafting for as long as I can remember and cannot look at any item without thinking about how I could adapt it for use in my home."

Jennifer Ulrick is a stay-at-home mom in Farmington, Minnesota. She's married to her high school sweetheart and has two energetic young boys. A graduate of the Savannah College of Art and Design, she applies her graphic-design knowledge to scrapbooking, card making, and other paper crafting. Prior to staying at home to raise her sons, she worked for Archiver's marketing department, developing workshops, creating store samples, and teaching classes.